Follow Me Around™
Italy

By Wiley Blevins

SCHOLASTIC

Content Consultant: David I. Kertzer, PhD, Paul Dupee University Professor of Social Science, Professor of Anthropology and Italian Studies, Brown University, Providence, Rhode Island

Library of Congress Cataloging-in-Publication Data
Names: Blevins, Wiley, author.
Title: Italy / by Wiley Blevins.
Description: New York, NY : Children's Press, 2018. | Series: Follow me around | Includes bibliographical references and index.
Identifiers: LCCN 2017030778 | ISBN 9780531234556 (library binding) | ISBN 9780531243671 (pbk.)
Subjects: LCSH: Italy—Juvenile literature. | Italy—Description and travel—Juvenile literature.
Classification: LCC DG417 .B585 2018 | DDC 945—dc23
LC record available at https://lccn.loc.gov/2017030778

Design: Judith Christ Lafond & Anna Tunick Tabachnik
Text: Wiley Blevins
© 2018 Scholastic Inc.

1 2 3 4 5 6 7 8 9 10 R 27 26 25 24 23 22 21 20 19 18

Photos ©: cover background: S.Borisov/Shutterstock; cover boy: Alistair Berg/Getty Images; back cover: Alistair Berg/Getty Images; 1: Alistair Berg/Getty Images; 3: VanWyckExpress/iStockphoto; 4 left: Alistair Berg/Getty Images; 6: Hercules Milas/Alamy Images; 7 right: Andreas von Einsiedel/Alamy Images; 7 left: Peter Horree/Alamy Images; 8 left: R, Ian Lloyd/Masterfile; 8 right: SerafinoMozzo/iStockphoto; 9 spaghetti: Floortje/iStockphoto; 9 lasagne: Andrii Gorulko/Shutterstock; 9 macaroni: viennetta/iStockphoto; 9 manicotti: CSP_mantonino/age fotostock; 9 conchiglie: George3973/Shutterstock; 9 penne: walterbilotta/iStockphoto; 9 vermicelli: LucianoBibulich/iStockphoto; 9 ruote: eyewave/iStockphoto; 9 farfalle: Floortje/iStockphoto; 9 rigatoni: alexandro900/Shutterstock; 9 capelli d'angelo: EugeneTomeev/iStockphoto; 9 linguini: Floortje/iStockphoto; 9 rotini: exopixel/Shutterstock; 9 fusilli: bergamont/Shutterstock; 10: MikeDotta/Shutterstock; 11: BoskoJr/iStockphoto; 12: Romulus and Remus, from 'The Children's Hour:Stories from the Classics', published by the Waverley Book Company (colour litho), Brock, Charles Edmund (1870-1938)/Private Collection/Bridgeman Art Library; 12-13 background: Vadim Yerofeyev/Dreamstime; 13: Romulus and Remus (gouache on paper), Baraldi, Severino (b.1930)/Private Collection/© Look and Learn/Bridgeman Art Library; 14 left: traveler1116/iStockphoto; 14 right: Simon Montgomery/robertharding/Getty Images; 15: IakovKalinin/iStockphoto; 16 top left: Ken Scicluna/AWL Images; 16 bottom: vitmore/iStockphoto; 16 top right-17 top left: leoks/Shutterstock; 17 top right: kavalenkava/Shutterstock; 17 bottom: Angelafoto/iStockphoto; 18 top: The Granger Collection; 18 bottom right: Archivart/Alamy Images; 18 bottom left: Ann Ronan Pictures/Print Collector/Getty Images; 19 top: Franco Origlia/Getty Images; 19 bottom left: Paul Fearn/Alamy Images; 19 bottom right: VincentDrago/Alamy Images; 20 bottom: Robbie Jack - Corbis/Getty Images; 20 top: The Granger Collection; 21 left: Kostyantyn Ivanyshen/Shutterstock; 21 right: Tinxi/Shutterstock; 21 center: KAZUHIRO NOGI/AFP/Getty Images; 22 left: TIZIANA FABI/AFP/Getty Images; 22-23 masks: Africa Studio/Shutterstock; 23 top right: RelaxFoto.de/iStockphoto; 23 center right top: Ken Scicluna/Getty Images; 23 center right bottom: Justin Setterfield/Getty Images; 23 bottom right: Odyssey-Images/Alamy Images; 24 left: Marco Iacobucci EPP/Shutterstock; 24 right-25 bottom left: Rodrigo Garrido/Shutterstock; 25 right: Dave G. Houser/Getty Images; 25 top left: Niyazz/iStockphoto; 26 left: Alberto Incrocci/Getty Images; 26 top right: Ed Freeman/Getty Images; 26 bottom right: Massimo Pizzotti/Getty Images; 27 top: Imgorthand/iStockphoto; 27 bottom left: SF photo/Shutterstock; 27 bottom right: VanWyckExpress/iStockphoto; 28 A: Fedor Selivanov/Shutterstock; 28 C: Anna_Om/iStockphoto; 28 E: SalvoV/iStockphoto; 28 D: JayBoivin/iStockphoto; 28 F: Levranii/Shutterstock; 28 G: Vova Pomortzeff/Alamy Images; 28 B: Giorgio Cosulich/Getty Images; 30 top right: chokkicx/iStockphoto; 30 top left: Leontura/iStockphoto; 30 bottom: Alistair Berg/Getty Images. Maps by Jim McMahon.

Table of Contents

Where in the World Is Italy?

Ciao (chow) from Italy! That's how we say "Hello." I'm Fausto, your tour guide. My name means "lucky." I hope someday you'll be lucky enough to visit my big and fascinating country.

Italy is located in southern Europe. Many people say it's shaped like a tall boot. Take a look. You can almost see it kicking the island of Sicily.

We have a special way to describe life in Italy: *la dolce vita*. That means "the sweet life." We Italians love to relax, enjoy life, and eat well. We also love soccer, my favorite sport ever! Now let me show you around our beautiful country for some fun.

Fast Facts:

- Italy is a <u>**peninsula**</u>, with seas on three sides.

- Italy includes Sicily and Sardinia, plus hundreds of other, smaller islands.

- Sicily is the largest island in the Mediterranean Sea. It is home to Mount Etna, an active volcano.

- **Much of Italy is covered in mountains. The Alps are in northern Italy, and the Apennines run all the way down the peninsula.**

- **The Po is Italy's longest river.**

- Italy covers 116,348 square miles (301,340 square kilometers).

- Italy's weather tends to be fairly cool in the north and warmer to the south. The east is dryer than the west.

5

People love eating outdoors in our trattoria.

Home Sweet Home

I am from Rome, Italy. In Italy, we believe "family is first," and our lives center on our families. I live with my parents, younger sister, and grandparents. If you visit my home, you won't be able to miss the delicious smells. My family owns and runs a *trattoria*, and we live in an apartment above it. A *trattoria* is a restaurant where you can dine on favorite local dishes, such as stuffed artichokes or grilled lamb. My family has always loved to cook. We especially love to eat with friends. So bring a big appetite!

Big windows and doorways let a lot of light into our apartment!

Sometimes we play soccer in the Piazza del Popolo (People's Square) near where I live.

My family's apartment is not big, but it is beautiful. Like most homes in Italy, most of our floors are tiled.

Family in Italy comes first, but friends are a close second. I've known some of my friends nearly all my life. We like to go to movies, grab a bite, practice our soccer skills, or just hang out at the *piazza*. A piazza is a public square.

Sometimes I go shopping with my parents. We usually go to a local supermarket. If you plan to go to a supermarket while you're here, be sure to bring your own bags. The store will charge you extra if you use theirs. And don't go in the middle of the day. A lot of stores close for lunch for a couple of hours.

Gelato

Each region in Italy has a particular way to cook their pizza.

Let's Eat!

Food is a big part of life in Italy. Breakfast is a small meal. I often eat only a roll with some jam on it. My parents have coffee with hot milk, a drink called *caffe latte*. That really wakes them up!

I eat my main meal for the day in the early afternoon when I return from school. It almost always includes pasta and some meat or fish. Everyone in my family gathers for this meal.

My family's evening meal is much lighter. We usually have cold cuts, or cold sliced meat, and cheese. On special days, we go to a restaurant and share a pizza! But be warned. We eat very late. Most restaurants don't open for dinner until 7:30 p.m. or later.

Of course, our favorite way to end a meal is with dessert. My family and I often go out for *gelato*, which is the Italian version of ice cream. At the gelato shop, you have lots of choices— fruit-flavored gelatos, chocolate, lemon, hazelnut, milk, and more. You'll have to try them all when you visit!

Pizza is my favorite snack, but I also love pasta! Italy is known for it. And there are so many different ways to prepare it! You can top it with *Bolognese*, a red sauce with meat. *Carbonara* is a creamy sauce made with eggs, cheese, and usually bacon. Try a simple tomato sauce such as *pomodoro*, or just add some olive oil and garlic.

Each Italian eats about 60 pounds (27 kilograms) of pasta a year! And boy, do we have lots of choices. Look at this chart to see the wide variety of pastas we enjoy.

Italy is also known for its tasty cheeses. Parmesan cheese comes from the Parma countryside in northern Italy. Mozzarella cheese comes from southern Italy. It was first made using the milk of water buffalo! We also eat a lot of olives, *salami*, and ham.

Pasta shapes

spaghetti

rigatoni

penne

lasagne

rotini

vermicelli

macaroni

capelli d'angelo

ruote

manicotti

linguini

farfalle

conchiglie

fusilli

We study most of the same subjects as kids do in other countries.

Let's Go to School

In Italy, we go to school six days a week. That's right—only one day off! But don't feel too bad for us. We get out early in the afternoon, usually around 1 o'clock. That gives us plenty of time to do all our homework.

We start school at age 6. We have to study hard because at age 14, we take an important test. This test determines which high school we will go to. Some kids go to a high school that prepares them for college. Others go to a high school where they prepare for a particular trade, or job.

Most of our school lessons are taught in Italian, our official language. We also study English as a second language. My older relatives speak French. It was the most common second language in Italy before we started using English.

The story of Pinocchio, a puppet that became a boy, is famous.

In school, we read a lot of tales, myths, and legends from long ago. The most popular fairy tale is Pinocchio. It's a story about a wooden puppet that magically turns into a real boy. What's even more unusual is that whenever Pinocchio tells a lie, his nose grows. Uh-oh! One of my favorite stories comes from Roman mythology. It is the myth about how my city of Rome began. It's the tale of Romulus and Remus.

Counting to 10

Knowing how to count to 10 is helpful when you visit Italy. Take 10 minutes and learn these numbers.

1	**uno** *(OO-noh)*
2	**due** *(DOO-ay)*
3	tre *(TRAY)*
4	**quattro** *(KWAH-troh)*
5	**cinque** *(CHEEN-kway)*
6	**sei** *(SAY-ee)*
7	**sette** *(SEH-tay)*
8	**otto** *(OHT-toh)*
9	nove *(NOH-vay)*
10	**dieci** *(dee-AY-cheeh)*

The Myth of Romulus and Remus

Long ago, a beautiful princess named Rhea married the god Mars. He was the god of war and very powerful. Soon after they married, the couple had twin boys and named them Romulus and Remus. The other gods were not happy about this marriage between a god and a human. The gods plotted to kill the two boys. To save her sons, Rhea placed the boys in a basket. Then she sent them floating down a river. They were found by a mother wolf, who decided to raise them as her own. The boys grew until the mother wolf could no longer care for them. One day, she hid them where she hoped a shepherd and his wife would find them. The couple did find them, and they raised the boys as their own.

When the boys became

men, they decided to build a city together. It would be a great city built on seven hills. The brothers had a contest to see which of them would be king of this grand new city. Remus was winning the contest until Romulus became so furious he did something awful. He killed Remus. Romulus became the first king of the city that he and his brother had dreamed of building. And what city was it? The city of Rome! Rome was named after **Rom**ulus. Since it was a city started by the son of a god, it was destined to become the most powerful and important city in all the land. And it did.

Trevi Fountain

Spanish Steps

Around My Big Country

Rome: Capital City

Welcome to my city, Rome. We call it Roma. It's the capital of Italy and our largest city. It has an interesting mix of modern and ancient buildings. Just turn the corner and you might find a building, statue, or fountain from long ago. One must-see fountain is the Trevi Fountain. It is the most famous fountain in the world! In the center is a statue of Oceanus, the god of the sea. I recommend you go at night to see it all lit up. Spectacular! You should also stop and take a photo at the Spanish Steps, which aren't too far away. With 135 steps, it's one of the largest and widest staircases in Europe and has an amazing view of Rome.

Colosseum

Eternal City

Rome is known as the Eternal City because of its long history. A must-see ancient site here is the Colosseum. It is an outdoor stadium and was built about 2,000 years ago. Romans would gather to watch **gladiators** battle it out in the Colosseum's arena. Today, you can tour this ancient building. Be on the lookout for cats. Big groups of them like to gather and play in many of Rome's ancient ruins.

Rome is a great city to walk around in, but you can also hop on our subway. We have two lines: the A line (red) and the B line (blue). If you want to leave the city, the train is an easy and fast way to travel.

It's All Latin to Me

The ancient Romans spoke Latin. This language is not spoken today, but it is still very useful. Many English words came from Latin. Also, many Latin words and phrases are used today.

vice versa to reverse the order of something

et cetera and so on (usually used at the end of a list that could go on)

status quo the current state or condition of something (as in keeping things "status quo" or the same)

mea culpa used when admitting your own guilt—like saying "my bad" or "my fault"

verbatim to repeat something word for word with no changes

alma mater the school you graduated from

Can you figure out this silly play on words my Latin teacher taught us?

Semper ubi sub ubi.

Hint: *semper* = always, *ubi* = where, *sub* = under.

Answer: Always wear underwear.

15

Gondoliers usually dress in a blue or red striped top, a red neckerchief, a wide-brimmed straw hat, and dark pants.

Venice: Magical Floating City

Venice is one of my favorite places in Italy. We call it Venezia. It is a port city, so lots of boats stop there. The city is built on more than 100 small islands. The buildings sit right next to the narrow **canals** that snake around the islands. It looks like the buildings—many of which are old palaces—are floating on the water! No cars are allowed. You get around by walking or taking a water bus, or *vaporetto,* up and down the Grand Canal. Tourists also love traveling around in gondolas, the narrow boats you'll also find there. Many of the drivers, or *gondoliers*, sing popular Italian songs as they row their oars.

Make sure you stop to see St. Mark's Basilica, the biggest church in Venice. Be careful, however, of going there during high tide. The city streets might be covered in water. Also, keep an eye out for lions with wings. They are the symbol of Venice and can be spotted on buildings everywhere.

Winged lion

Amalfi Coast

The Duomo in Florence

Italian City Names

Roma	–	Rome
Genova	–	Genoa
Milano	–	Milan
Firenze	–	Florence
Napoli	–	Naples
Torino	–	Turin

Other Fun Places to Visit

Naples is a major seaport and our third-largest city. We call it Napoli. Greeks founded the city in the 600s BCE. Naples is famous for its puppet theaters. In fact, one of the symbols of Naples is a silly-looking puppet named Pulcinella with a large curved nose. You can't miss it. The puppet wears oversized white clothes and a black mask.

After you visit Naples, drive down the Amalfi Coast. It is one of the most beautiful drives in the world. But be careful. You'll see the hillside on one side of the narrow, curvy road and the sea on the other! You'll need a strong stomach to look out the car windows on this ride.

You should also see Florence, or Firenze, at the heart of the region of Tuscany. If you like architecture, stop by the Duomo, or cathedral, with its red-tiled dome. The city's museums offer stunning examples of paintings, sculptures, and other creations. And don't miss the chance to take a walk along the Arno River.

Pulcinella

Our Fascinating History

Thousands of years ago, Italy began as a collection of little villages. One of these villages was Rome. It was founded on the banks of the Tiber River in 753 BCE. The village grew and eventually became the heart of the Roman **Empire**. Romans ruled parts of Europe, Africa, and Asia for hundreds of years. Many famous emperors ruled during these years, including Augustus Caesar.

Ancient Rome

A painting by Renaissance artist Piero dell Francesca

Augustus Caesar

Timeline: Italy's History

753 BCE	**509 BCE**	**27 BCE–476 CE**	**1300s–1500s**
Birth of Rome The city of Rome is established.	**Roman Republic** Elected officials help create the Roman Republic.	**Roman Empire** The Roman Empire rules lands from Europe to Africa to Asia.	**Renaissance** Great advances in learning and art take place in and around what is now Italy.

Historically, Italy is known as the seat, or center, of the Roman Catholic religion. And nowhere is this more important than in Vatican City. It is located inside the city of Rome and is the home of the pope, the leader of the Roman Catholic Church. Vatican City is a separate country—the smallest in the world. About 800 people live there. That's it!

Pope Francis poses for a selfie.

Benito Mussolini

1871

Kingdom of Italy
Following many wars, several separate Italian states unite.

1922–1943

Mussolini
Benito Mussolini rules Italy. He was elected prime minister in 1922 and declared himself dictator, with full power, in 1925.

1939–1945

World War II
Italy and Germany fight and lose to Great Britain, the United States, the Soviet Union, and their allies.

1946

Italian Republic
The Italian Republic forms.

It Came From Italy

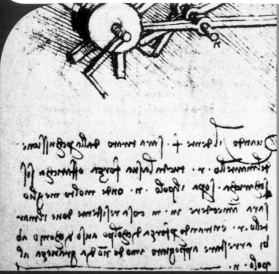

One of the most important Italian artists was Leonardo da Vinci. His most famous artworks include *Mona Lisa* and *The Last Supper*. He was a great thinker and inventor, as well. He often wrote notes backwards. We call this "mirror writing." Hold a mirror near this note and see what happens!

Italian opera is a traditional art form. In an opera, the actors sing their lines instead of saying them. Operas are known for their drama-filled stories that feature things such as big palaces, troops on horseback, acrobats, and long death scenes. Almost every large city in Italy has an opera house.

Italy has some of the most luxurious cars in the world. Hop in a Ferrari with your parents and you'll feel like a million bucks! Other luxury cars made in Italy include the Lamborghini and Maserati. Vroom!

Many famous world explorers came from Italy. Marco Polo traveled as far as China and Indonesia in the 13th century. Christopher Columbus accidentally landed on an island in the Caribbean Sea near North America. Amerigo Vespucci sailed across the Atlantic Ocean not long after. The word *America* comes from his name.

We Italians take great pride in how we dress. As the heart of our fashion **industry**, Milan is home to many famous clothing designers. We work to look our best at all times. So bring some nice clothes to wear when you go out to eat at night.

Women in Viterbo dress as la Befana in the town's annual procession.

Make a Carnival Mask

Materials:
Sheet of paper, sheet of cardstock or cardboard, small stick (such as a popsicle stick), scissors, glue and tape, decorations (markers, paint, glitter, feathers, etc.)

Let's Celebrate!

Everyone loves a holiday, and we have some fun ones in Italy. Christmas is my favorite. We celebrate it from December 24 through January 6—much longer than in some other countries. The last day of this celebration is a special one. You'll see lots of girls dressed as *la Befana*, a witch. This witch brings presents, so we like her a lot!

1 To make your mask template, fold the paper in half. Draw half a mask. Make sure the middle of the mask touches the folded edge. This way, when you unfold the paper, you'll have a full mask! It can be any shape—a star, a butterfly, or the more common design above.

2 Cut out the mask template.

February March

March April

June

July August

3 Lay the template on the cardstock or cardboard. Trace around the template. Cut out your mask. Be careful with the eyeholes.

4 Decorate your mask. Have fun!

5 Tape the small stick to one side of the mask.

You're done! Find a mirror, put on your mask, and enjoy.

Carnival: Our most famous Carnival celebration is in Venice, where people roam the streets wearing masks and outfits in styles from the 1400s. Carnival occurs each year before Lent, a time when people give up one thing (such as eating chocolate) in the six weeks leading up to Easter.

Easter: This is our most important religious holiday. We go to church on Sunday and then take Monday off work and school to relax with our families.

Calcio Fiorentino: Celebrated on June 24, this honors John the Baptist, the patron saint of Florence. It is celebrated by playing an older version of soccer. In fact, *calcio* is the Italian word for "soccer." How is calcio different? Teams dressed in special colorful costumes can punch and elbow each other. Rough!

Palio di Siena: This ancient horse race is still run through the streets of Siena today. It takes place on July 2 and August 16. Each city district has a horse. The winner is the pride of Siena!

soccer

Formula One is sometimes shortened to F1.

Time to Play

Kids in Italy love soccer—including me. We call it the king of sports! My friends and I cram into crowded, noisy stadiums to cheer on our favorite team. We're so good at soccer we've even won the World Cup, the biggest international competition, several times. Most big cities in Italy have at least one team, and there are matches all the time. When not watching soccer, my friends and I are playing it. Our soccer stars are national heroes, much like the gladiators from ancient Rome.

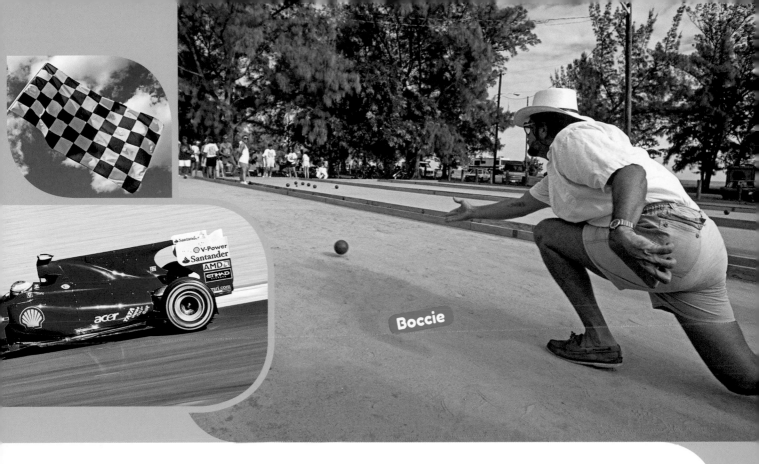

Boccie

Sports are a popular pastime in Italy. Basketball, cycling, Formula One racing, skiing, skating, swimming, and *boccie* are favorites. Boccie is lawn bowling. It takes a steady hand and a good eye to win. Formula One racing is a must to see in person. The cars are low to the ground and super fast. My favorite Formula One race is the Italian Grand Prix. Round and round the racers go until they see the checkered flag that means the race is over.

You Won't Believe This!

Italy has produced many renowned artists, such as Michelangelo. He created many different types of art. He created beautiful statues, such as a statue of David. He also made fresco paintings on walls and ceilings of churches. His painting on the ceiling of the Sistine Chapel in Vatican City is one of them. He painted some of it while lying on his back! You can see his works there and in museums here and around the world.

Mount Vesuvius

Italy has several large volcanoes, the most in all of Europe. Why? Italy sits on a major **fault line**. That's where the giant plates under the ground, called tectonic plates, meet. When they push against, pull away from, or slide past each other, earthquakes and volcanic eruptions happen.

Most Italians don't work in August. There's a two-week period called *ferragosto* during the Feast of the Assumption of the Virgin holiday. Most businesses are closed these weeks. Many Italians take the whole month off for vacation. Yay! My family goes to the beach not far from Rome for some fun in the sun.

Italy has not one, but two small countries inside it. The Republic of San Marino is one of them. It covers just 24 square miles (62 sq km). Vatican City is the other. It covers only 0.17 square miles (0.44 sq km).

Vatican City

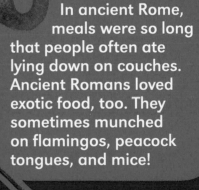

In ancient Rome, meals were so long that people often ate lying down on couches. Ancient Romans loved exotic food, too. They sometimes munched on flamingos, peacock tongues, and mice!

Guessing Game!

Here are some other great sites around Italy. If you have time, try to see them all!

Italy's largest active volcano, this is found on the island of Sicily.

E

1. Catacombs of Rome
2. Mount Etna
3. Sardinia beaches
4. Pompeii ruins
5. Leaning Tower of Pisa
6. Cinque Terre National Park
7. Aquarium of Genoa

A

This famous marble building was built on soft land between the 12th and 14th centuries. It now tilts about 16 feet (5 meters) to the side.

F

Have fun in the sun on these great beaches. You can also spot a rare albino donkey, ride a horse, enjoy water sports, learn to dive, and much more.

B

If you're feeling brave, explore these underground Roman tombs, which contain the remains of people from long ago.

Explore a variety of sea life at this large port-city aquarium.

G

This national park consists of five small towns nestled on cliffs overlooking the sea.

C

D

This city was covered in ash when Mount Vesuvius erupted in 79 CE. Although it remained covered for centuries, today tourists can roam the ancient streets of this ghost town.

How to Prepare for Your Visit

By now, you should be ready to hop on a plane to Italy. Here are some tips to prepare for your trip.

❶ Before you come to Italy, exchange your money. Our money is called the euro, which we use as a member of the European Union. Look on the one-euro coin and you'll see a famous drawing by Italian artist Leonardo da Vinci.

❷ Don't be surprised if Italians talk with you in an animated way. We speak as much with our hands as with words. Hand gestures help deliver our message.

❸ You'll be doing a lot of walking in Italy, so bring some comfortable shoes. Make sure they are slip-proof. You'll be walking on old stone streets and maybe even up the side of a volcano. Also, you'll probably visit many churches. You need to dress appropriately. Wear long pants or skirts and shirts that cover your shoulders (no tank tops).

❹ Need a bite to eat? You'll have many options. In a *paninoteca*, you can grab a quick sandwich. Feast on a traditional dinner in an *osteria*. If you aren't super hungry, don't worry. Order a *mezzo piatto*, or half portion. Want just a slice of pizza? Our *pizzerie* use wood-fired ovens and offer lots of topping choices.

❺ Bring a converter, a special type of plug-in, for your electronics. Otherwise, your phone or tablet charger won't fit into the outlet. Not good!

The United States Compared to Italy

Official Name	United States of America (USA)	Italian Republic
Official Language	No official language, though English is most commonly used	Italian
Population	325 million	Almost 61 million
Common Words	yes; **no**; good morning; **please**; thank you	sì (see); **no**; buon giorno (bwon ZHOR-no); **prego** (PREH-goh); grazie (GRAHT-zee-ay)
Flag		
Money	Dollar	Euro
Location	North America	Europe
Highest Point	Denali (Mount McKinley)	Mont Blanc (in the Alps)
Lowest Point	Death Valley	Mediterranean Sea (near Ferrara)
National Anthem	"The Star-Spangled Banner"	"Fratelli d'Italia"

So now you know some important and fascinating things about my country, Italy. I hope to see you someday exploring one of our popular cities, taking a photo at one of our ancient ruins, or eating at my family's trattoria in Rome. Until then . . . *arrivederci* (ah-ree-vuh-DEHR-chee)! Good-bye!

Glossary

canals
(kuh-NALZ)
channels that are dug across land so boats or ships can travel between two bodies of water, or so water can flow from one place to another

empire
(EM-pire)
a group of countries or states that have the same ruler

fault line
(FAWLT LINE)
a large break in the earth's surface where an earthquake might happen

gladiators
(GLAD-ee-ay-turz)
people in ancient Rome who fought other people or wild animals, often to the death, to provide entertainment

industry
(IN-duh-stree)
a single area of business or trade

peninsula
(puh-NIN-suh-luh)
a piece of land that sticks out from a larger landmass and is almost completely surrounded by water

Index

Facts for Now

Visit this Scholastic website for more information on Italy and to download the Teaching Guide for this series:

www.factsfornow.scholastic.com   Enter the keyword **Italy**

About the Author

Wiley Blevins is an author living and working in New York City. His greatest love is traveling, and he has been to Italy many times. He finds Venice to be one of the most magical, jaw-dropping cities on earth. Wiley has written numerous books for kids, including other books in the Follow Me Around series.